YOUR KNOWLEDGE HAS

Saravana Kumar, Naveen Kumar

Optimized Ranking-Based Techniques for Improving Aggregate Recommendation Diversity

GRIN Publishing

Bibliographic information published by the German National Library:

The German National Library lists this publication in the National Bibliography; detailed bibliographic data are available on the Internet at http://dnb.dnb.de .

Imprint:

Copyright © 2013 GRIN Verlag GmbH
Print and binding: Books on Demand GmbH, Norderstedt Germany
ISBN: 978-3-656-56324-2

This book at GRIN:

http://www.grin.com/en/e-book/266178/optimized-ranking-based-techniques-for-improving-aggregate-recommendation

GRIN - Your knowledge has value

Since its foundation in 1998, GRIN has specialized in publishing academic texts by students, college teachers and other academics as e-book and printed book. The website www.grin.com is an ideal platform for presenting term papers, final papers, scientific essays, dissertations and specialist books.

Visit us on the internet:

http://www.grin.com/

http://www.facebook.com/grincom

http://www.twitter.com/grin_com

Optimized Ranking-Based Techniques for Improving Aggregate Recommendation Diversity

SARAVANAKUMAR A
SBM College of Engineering & Technology,

NAVEENKUMAR.N
SBM College of Engineering & Technology,

ABSTRACT:
This paper investigates how demand-side factors contribute to the Internet's "Long Tail" phenomenon. It first models how a reduction in search costs will affect the concentration in product sales. Then, by analyzing data collected from a multi-channel retailing company, it provides empirical evidence that the Internet channel exhibits a significantly less concentrated sales distribution, when compared with traditional channels. The difference in the sales distribution is highly significant, even after controlling for consumer differences. Furthermore, the effect is particularly strong for individuals with more prior experience using the Internet channel. We find evidence that Internet purchases made by consumers with prior Internet experience are more skewed toward obscure products, compared with consumers who have no such experience. We observe the opposite outcome when comparing purchases by the same consumers through the catalog channel. If the relationships we uncover persist, the underlying trends in technology and search costs portend an ongoing shift in the distribution of product sales.Singular Value Decomposition (SVD), together with the Expectation-Maximization (EM) procedure, can be used to find a low-dimension model that maximizes the loglikelihood of observed ratings in recommendation systems. However, the computational cost of this approach is a major concern, since each iteration of the EM algorithm requires a new SVD computation. We present a novel algorithm that incorporates SVD approximation into the EM procedure to reduce the overall computational cost while maintaining accurate predictions. Furthermore, we propose a new framework for collaborating filtering in distributed recommendation systems that allows users to maintain their own rating profiles for privacy. We conduct o_ine and online tests of our ranking algorithm. For o_ine testing, we use Yahoo! Search queries that resulted in a click on a Yahoo! Movies or Internet Movie Database (IMDB) movie URL. Our online test involved 44 Yahoo! Employees providing subjective assessments of results quality. In both tests, our ranking methods show signi_cantly better recall and quality than IMDB search and Yahoo! Movies current search. Reduced rank approximation of matrices has hitherto been possible only by unweighted least squares. This paper presents iterative techniques for obtaining such approximations when weights are introduced. The techniques involve criss-cross regressions with careful initialization. Possible applications of the approximation are in modeling, biplotting, contingency table analysis, fitting of missing values, checking outliers, etc.

1. Introduction

Collaborative Filtering analyzes a user preferences database to predict additional products or services in which a user might be interested. The goal is to predict the preferences of a user based on the preferences of others with similar tastes. There are two general classes of collaborative filtering algorithms. Low-dimension linear models are a popular means to describe user preferences. The following are representative state-of-the-art collaborative filtering algorithms.directly assume that the user preferences database is generated from a linear model, matrix factorization based collaborative filtering methods obtain an explicitlinear model to approximate the original user preferences matrix, and use the Pearson correlation coefficient, which is equivalent to a linear fit. If we assume that users' ratings are generated from a low-dimension linear model together with Gaussiandistributed noise, the Singular Value Decomposition (SVD) technique can be used to find the linear model that maximizes the log-likelihood of the rating matrix, assuming it is complete. If the rating matrix is incomplete, as is the case in real-world systems, SVD cannot be applied directly. The Expectation-Maximization (EM) procedure can be used to find the model that maximizes the log-likelihood of the available ratings, but this requires a SVD computation of the whole matrix for each EM iteration. As the size of the rating matrix is usually huge (due to large numbers of users and items in typical recommendation systems), the computational cost of SVD becomes an important concern. Deterministic SVD methods for computing all singular vectors on anm-by-n matrix take $O(mn2+m2n)$ time, and the Lanczos method requires roughly $O(kmn \log(mn))$ time to approximate the top k singular vectors [10]. In this work, we present a novel algorithm based on using an SVD approximation.

There are several challenges for adapting item authority in these information retrieval systems due to the di_erent characteristics of documents like item or product informa-tion documents in commercial sites, as compared to web documents. The power of PageRank and HITS stems from the feature of links between web documents. PageRank and HITS assume that a link from document i to j represents a recommendation or endorsement of document j by the owner of document i. However, in item information pages in commercial sites, links often represent di_erent kinds of relationships other than recommendation. For example, two items may be linked because both items are produced by the same company. Also, since these item information pages are generally created by providers rather than users or cus-tomers, the documents may contain the providers' perspec-tive on the items rather than those of users or customers. On the other hand, recommender systems are widely used in ecommerce sites to overcome information overload. Note that information retrieval systems work somewhat passively while recommender systems look for the need of a user more actively.

2. RELATEDWORK
Recommender systems can be built in three ways:
content-based _ltering, collaborative _ltering, and hybrid systems.Content-based recommender systems, sometimes called in-formation _ltering systems, use behavioral user data for a single user in order to try to infer the types of item attributes that the user is interested in. Collaborative _ltering compares one user's behavior against a database of other users' behaviors in order to identify items that like-minded users are interested in. Even though content-based recommender

systems are e_cient in _ltering out unwanted information and generating recommendations for a user from massive information, they _nd few if any coincidental discoveries. On the other hand, collaborative _ltering systems enables serendipitous discoveries by using historical user data.

Collaborative _ltering algorithms range from simple nearest neighbor methods to more complex machine learning based methods such as graph based methods linear algebra based methods and probabilistic methods. A few variations of lterbot based algorithms and hybrid methods that combine content and a collaborative ltering have also been proposed to attack the so-called cold start problem.Tapestry is one of the earliest recommender systems.In this system, each user records their opinions (annota-tions) of documents they read, and these annotations are accessed by others' _lters. GroupLens4, Ringo and Video Recommender are the earliest fully automatic recommender systems, which provide recommendations of news, music, and movies. PHOAKS (People Helping One Another Know Stu_) crawls web messages and extracts recommendations from them rather than using users' explicit ratings. GroupLens has also developed a movie recommender system called MovieLens5. Fab is the _rst hybrid recommender system, which use a combination of content-based and collaborative _ltering techniques for web recommendations. Tango provides online news recommendations and Jester provides recommendations of jokes. A new concept of document relevance, often called document authority, and developed the PageRank and HITS algorithms, respectively, for better precision in web search. Both algorithms analyze the link structure of the Web to calculate document authorities. Haveliwala proposed topic sensitive PageRank, which generates multiple document authorities biased to each speci_c topic for better document ranking.Note that our approach is di_erent from general web search engines since we use user ratings rather than link structure for generating item authorities. Also, our approach is di_erent from topic-sensitive PageRank since we provide personalized item authorities for each user rather than topic-biased item authorities. Also, our approach is di_erent from recommender systems since it uses predictions of items as a ranking function for information search rather than generating recommendation.

3. SVD Approximation in Centralized Recommendation Systems

In this section, we discuss how to use SVD approximation to reduce the computational cost of the SVD based collaborative filtering in traditional centralized recommendation systems where the server keeps all users' rating profiles. If the server uses the EM procedure shown in Section 2, the computational cost will be $1 \cdot O(mn2 + m2n)$, in which 1 is the number of iterations of the EM procedure and $O(mn2+m2n)$ is the computational cost of performing deterministicSVD on an m(users)-by-n(items) matrix. This cost is expensive because m and n can be very large in a recommendation system, from thousands to millions. The SVD Approximation technique of Drineas et $al.$ shows that for any matrix A (m-by-n), if c rows are sampled and scaled appropriately, the top right singular vectors of the new matrix C (c-by-n) approximate the top right singular vectors of A. More formally, assume that in picking a certain row for C, the probability that the ith row in A is picked (denoted as pi) is such that pi $\geq$ $\beta\_A(i)\_2/\_A\_2F$, where β is a constant and $\_ \cdot \_$, denoting a vector's length, is equal to the squared root of the sum of the squares of all its elements, and suppose that if A(i) is picked, $A(i)/\sqrt{c}p_i$ will be included as a row in C. Denote H (n-by-k) as the matrix formed by the top k right singular vectors of C and Ak (Ak = $U_kS_kV^T{}_k$) as the best rank k approximation to A. It follows that for any $c \le n$ and $\delta > 0$, $A-AHHT\_2F\le$ $\_A-Ak\_2F +2(1+\_8$ $\ln(2/\delta))\_k\beta c\_A\_2F$.(2)In addition, if $p_i = \_A(i)\_2/\_A\_2F$, which implies that β isequal to one,$\_A-AHHT\_2F\le \_A-Ak\_2F +2(1+\_8$ $n(2/\delta))\_kc\_A\_2F$.(3) The proof of both inequalities can be found in [5].As discussed in Section 2, the objective of the maximization step in the tth iteration of the EM procedure is to compute the best rank k approximation to the filled-in matrix A(t). Using SVD approximation, the server can sample c users' rating profiles (rows in A) with probability proportional to their length squared and form the matrix C after scaling. Note here that the c samples are not necessarily from c different users, and that a user's rating profile might be sampled more than once according to the sampling method. After computing the top k right singular vectors of C and obtaining the matrix H, the server can use A(t)HHT to approximate A(t) k . Then in the expectation step of the (t + 1)th iteration, the unknown entry Aij is calculated as (A(t)HHT)ij . By inequality (3), the server has a high confidence that given the same filled-in matrix A(t), the rank k model A(t)HHT obtained *via* SVD approximation is close to the best rank k approximation A(t) k . Therefore, with a high probability, the EM procedure is likely to calculate more and more likely true values for missing entries. This implies that although the EM procedure with SVD approximation is not guaranteed to converge on an optimal solution, the loglikelihood of observed ratings will generally increase.

Algorithm 1
EM Procedure *via* SVD approximation

1: Set initial values X(0) ij for unknown entries Aij .
2: **while** in the tth iteration of EM procedure **do**
3: Fill in A by replacing unknown entries Aij with X(t−1) ij , denote the filled-in matrix as A(t). 4: Set pi = _A(t) (i)_2/_A(t)_2 F , and pick c rows from A. If the ith row is picked, include A(t) (i)/√cpi in C.
5: Compute the top k right singular vectors of C and form hese k vectors into the matrix H.
6: X(t) = A(t)HHT .
7: **end while**

4. SVD Approximation in Distributed Recommendation Systems
Traditional centralized recommendation systems have problems such as users losing their privacy, retail monopolies being favored, and diffusion of innovations being hampered, Distributed collaborative filtering systems, where users keep their rating profiles to themselves, have the potential to correct these problems. However, in the distributed scenario there are two new problems that need to be dealt with. The first problem is how to ensure that users'data are not revealed to the server and other users. The second problem is how to ensure that users can get as accurate predictions as they do in the centralized scenario. This paper is mainly focused on the second problem, and consequently we rely mechanisms shown in to address the first problem.Since the server cannot directly see users' rating profiles, it needs to compute an *aggregate* (a learning result based on user information) for making predictions. Figure 1 shows our framework for collaborative filtering in distributed recommendation systems. At a certain time point t, the server securely computes the aggregate (denoted as Gt) from those users who are online at that time point (denoted as Ut); "securely" here means

that users' rating profiles are not disclosed to the server and other users. Between time point t and t + 1, when a certain user (no matter whether she is in Ut or not) needs predictions, the server computes predictions based on this user's rating profile and the aggregate Gt. The reason of computing aggregates periodically is that users' rating profiles are dynamic. For any given user, the probability that he is in Ut is independent of the probability that he is in Ut+1, so Ut and Ut+1 would be expected to

have few users in common (given sufficiently many users). Therefore, it is hard to find a way to combine aggregates computed at different time points for predictions. A more minor concern in this framework is how the server picks time points for aggregate computations.

4.1 Algorithms and Theoretical Analysis

We first present algorithms for computing aggregates and generating predictions and then a theoretical analysis of their performance. Assume that there are c online users at time point t, and that their rating profiles are denoted A(1) to A(c). Algorithm 2 shows how to generate the aggregate.

Algorithm 2

Computing the aggregate Gt

1: **for** each user i, to each unknown entry Aij **do**

2: If Aij has been predicted before, replace Aij with the latest prediction.

3: Else replace Aij with the average of user i's ratings.

4: **end for**

5: The server securely performs SVD on the matrix C (cby-n) formed by filled-in rating profiles.

6: Aggregate Gt is the matrix (n-by-c) formed by the top k right singular vectors of C.

Algorithm 3

Generating predictions for user i

1: For each unknown entry Aij, if Aij has been predicted before, replace Aij with the latest prediction.

2: Else replace Aij with the average of user i's ratings.

3: Multiply the filled-in rating profile vector (1-by-n) by GtGTt to generate predictions.

For analysis, we make the following two assumptions.

Assumption 1: there exists a constant β such that for any m and for any user i, the filled-in rating profile (denoted as A (i)) satisfies $\sum_{j=1}^{m}$ _A (j) _2/(m · _A (i) _2) ≥ β. Recall thatmis the total number of users

4.2 Stability of Predictions:

A potential problem in a rating system is that users, items, and ratings are all dynamic and subject to change at any time. As a result of this, the rating matrix may change between two aggregate computations as a result of the following three situations: 1) users giving new (updated) ratings on items; 2) new users being registered in the system; and 3) new items being added to the system. An altered rating matrix typically requires a different linear model to best describe it. However, the linear model should not be disturbed to a significant extent when the rating matrix undergoes a small change— otherwise predictions made between two aggregate computation will probably be inaccurate. Since the computed aggregate in Algorithm 2 approximates the top k right singular vectors (Vk) of the current filled-in rating matrix, the core concern is an instability in VkV T k . We conducted two preliminary experiments on a 5000- by-1427 rating matrix from the EachMovie data set to assess the impact of rating matrix changes on VkV T k . In the first experiment, 90% of the entries are randomly picked to form the original rating matrix A, and the rest of the entries are progressively added to form A^. In the second experiment, rating profiles from 90% of the users are used to form the initial matrix A and the remaining users are progressively added to create A^. The case where new items are added is not considered here because the size of VkV T k will change as the number of items is changed, and this will make it difficult to assess its effect. Figure 2 shows that the difference between VkV T

k and ^ Vk ^ V T k is in a small range (6%) when the number of rating cases or the number of users is increased within a small range (3%). In a real system, it is reasonable that changes in the number of rating cases and the number of users will be in this range between two consecutive aggregate computations.

4.3 Preserving Privacy

This work is not focused on improvements in preserving privacy in the distributed scenario, so to address the privacy issue in Algorithm 2 and 3, we apply security schemes proposed. In Algorithm 2, a distributed secure SVD computation is needed to ensure that users' rating profiles are not revealed to other users or the server. Canny's paper proposed a scheme to achieve this objective. The idea is to reduce the SVD computation to an iterative calculation requiring only the addition of vectors of user data, and use homomorphic encryption to allow the sums of encrypted vectors to be computed and decrypted without exposing individual data. In Algorithm 3, the multiplication of a user's rating profile by GtGTt should be securely computed both so that the server cannot learn the rating profile and so that the user cannot learn GtGTt . Moreover, the multiplication result should not be revealed to the server either, as in that case the server could easily compute the user's rating data. The multiplications of a vector by a matrix can be considered as a group of scalar products. There are several privacy preserving schemes for calculating

scalar products in the security literature and one of them is presented in. It also has an asymmetric version to let only one side know the final result.

5. RANKING ALGORITHM

Note that we only focus on movie title search rather than people (actor or director) search in our study. Thus, the term \item" is equivalent to \movie" or \movie title". Like general web search engines, our ranking algorithm consists of two main components: item proximity and item authority.

5.1 Item proximity: DB and Web relevance

5.1.1. DB relevance

Most movie search engines index only titles or few keywords on items. Thus, item relevance for the given query against a database are often measured by relevances of titles and keywords for the query. In other words, they are most useful when users already know what they are looking for. Search queries are assumed to be part of movie titles, or names of actors or directors. We de_ne these type of queries as navigational queries. However, when a user searches for something, in many cases he does not know much about the object, and that is one of main reasons why he searches for it. Sometimes, searching means trying to _nd unknown (or unfamiliar) information, which may be interesting. Thus, search tools should anticipate that some queries will be ambiguous or inexact. Even for niche search engines, the situation is not changed. Imagine a scienti_c literature search. Even though a scientist is very familiar with her research _eld, sometimes she is searching for articles that she might have missed. In this case, we cannot expect that she already knows the titles of the articles she is looking for.

Table 1:

	TF		TFIDF	
	HIT	No Returns	HIT	No Returns
IMDB	4	2	6	2
current Yahoo!	2	94	2	95
DB	33	25	37	43

Hit ratios of three movie search engines for the top 100 most popular movies; Only the top 10 returned movies are considered. \DB" denotes our base system with an extensive index. Two top TF/TFIDF terms from _ve metadata, including names of actors, directors, characters, plots, and genres, are selected as a query for each movie in the top 100 popular movies. Then each query is submitted to three systems, IMDB, Yahoo! Movies and our base system. The popularities of movies are measured by the number of user ratings. We downloaded the IMDB movie content data and conductedthis test in April 2006.

Table 2:
The e_ect of web relevance. \jlo" is submitted to each system as a query. Bold represents items relevant to Jennifer Lopez. The results are as of April 2006.

System	Top 10 movie results
Yahoo!	No returns
IMDB	1. Fejlvs (1968) 2. Mihajlo Bata Paskodjevic (2001) 3. Mihajlo Petrovic Alas (1968) 4. Mijlocus le deschidere (1979) 5. Scopul si mijloacele (1983) 6. A Szr s gykr fejkbe (1961) 7. Ziveo zivot Tola Manojlovic (1973) 8. Kunmonosn j (1957) 9. The Hello Country (1998) 10. Vlemma tou Odvssea, To (1995)
DB	No returns
Web	1. **Maid in Manhattan (2002)** A+ 2. **Angel Eyes (2001)** A- 3. **Let's Dance (1950)** B+ 4. Sweet 15 (1996) B+ 5. **My Family (1995)** B+ 6. **U-Turn (1997)** B+ 7. **The Cell (2000)** B 8. **The Wedding Planner (2001)** C-

5.2 Item authority
5.2.1 Global item authorities
We generate global item authorities. The global item authorities can be generated based on the items' average ratings over all users. However, we add some heuristics for calculating global item authorities, which emphasize both the popularity and quality of items. Note that the quality of items do not always match with the need of users. For example, even though some old movies have very good quality, most users may not look for those 40's or 50's movies since they prefer recently produced movies. In fact, only 57 users in our database have rated Citizen Kane (1941). Thus, we calculate global item authorities using the following equation:

$$Auth_i = r_i + \log_j U_{ij} + c_i + \log_{10}(10 \_ aw_i + 5 \_ an_i) \_ (3)$$

where U_i is the set of users who have rated item i over all users, r_i is the average rating of item i, c_i is the average critic rating of item i, aw_i is the number of awards that item i has won, an_i is the number of awards that item i has been nominated for, and _ is a normalization factor such that the maximum global item authority is . Also, we set such that the maximum value of $\log_j U_{ij}$ is 13. We use award scores and average critic ratings on items for assigning better authorities to the classic movies than the movies of which users have frequently rated but their average ratings are low.

5.2.2 Personal item authorities: Prediction
We use an item-based collaborative _ltering (CF) algorithm to calculate a user's expected ratings on the returned items. We have tested several collaborative _ltering algorithms including user-based CF and a few machine Table 3: Weak & strong generalization: The average normalized mean absolute errors and standard deviations on three sample sets are shown. Smaller numbers (lower errors) are better.

5.3 MADRank:

Our ranking system We assign item authorities for each search result based on the following procedure. We assign global item authorities as item authorities when the target user is unknown. When a user logs in our system, we partition returned items in each search result into two groups: items which the user has rated and others that the user has not rated. We assign the user's own ratings as item authorities for the _rst group and the user's expected ratings calculated by item-based algorithm for the second group. If we cannot calculate the user's expected ratings for any items in the second group due to lack of information, global item authorities are assigned for those items. Then the ranking score of document i for the given query q and user u is: MADRank(i; q; u) = _ _ Auth(i; q; u) + (1 _) _ Prox(i; q) (7) where _ is an weighting factor for item authorities. We set _ = 0:5. In addition, we set the MADRank score to 13 if the title of an item exactly matches to the given query. Table 4 shows the top 10 title search results of six movie search systems, including the current Yahoo! Movies search, IMDB search, and four of our own search systems, for the query \arnold action". DB denotes one variant of our systems with an extensive index and DB relevance based ranking. Web denotes a system using the Yahoo! Search API and web relevance ranking. GRank denotes a system using MADRank as a ranking system and item authorities are based on global item authorities. PRank denotes a system with MADRank and personal item authorities. Table 5 shows the pro_le of the test user used in the PRank. Note that the current Yahoo! Movies search does not return any titles due to AND matching within a limited index. IMDB does not return any Arnold Schwarzenneger movies in the top ten results. In the DB system, Arnold Schwarzenneger DVD 2-Pack - The Sixth Day/The Last Action Hero(2003) is shown _rst since the title contains both \arnold" and \action". However, the results still show the need of better ranking for informational search since many famous titles such as Terminator (1984) and Terminator 2: Judgment Day (1991) do not appear in the _rst search results. The result of Web seems to be better than that of DB. Note that several famous Schwarzenneger movies including Terminator (1984) and Terminator 3 (2003) appear in the top 10 results. However, Arnold Schwarzenneger DVD 2-Pack (2003) is still shown _rst. Several items including Terminator (1984) and Terminator 2 (1991) are boosted in the GRank due to their higher item authorities while Arnold Schwarzenneger DVD 2-Pack (2003) disappears from the top 10 due to its low global item authority. In PRank, Terminator (1984), Terminator 2 (1991) and Total Recall (1990) are boosted further since either the user has rated the items higher or his expected ratings for those items are high. Similarly, Terminator 3 (2003), Eraser (1996) and End of Days (1999) disappear due to their low personalized item authorities. By applying item authorities in the ranking function, we believe that search results can be signi_cantly improved.

6. OFFLINE EVALUATION:

We measure the e_ectiveness of our ranking algorithms by comparing against two existing systems|IMDB search and the current Yahoo! Movies search|in both online and o_ine tests. In this section, we discuss our o_ine test. We use search click data from Yahoo! Search containing search queries and clicked URLs. We select data stored on the _rst day of each month from October 2005 to May 2006. We extract all queries that resulted in a click on a movie page in either IMDB or Yahoo! Movies. Specically, we extract queries containing clicked-URLs starting with imdb.com/title or http://movies.yahoo.com/shop?d=hv. We use some heuristics to extract additional movie pages Table 4: Top 10 results of di_erent ranking methods for the query \arnold action". The results are as of April 2006.

7. ONLINE EVALUATION:

We also conduct an online evaluation using MAD6 [20], our prototype personalized movie earch and browsing engine. In this section, we _rst briey explain MAD6, then discuss our online test procedure and results.

7.1 MAD6 architecture

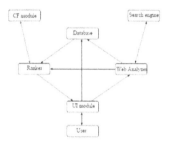

Figure 1: The architecture of MAD6.

The architecture of MAD6 is shown in Figure 1. It has four internal components (User Interface (UI) Module, Database, Web Analyzer and Ranker) and two external components (Search Engine and Collaborative Filtering (CF) Module). Note that the two external components are modular and can be exchanged with other systems. The User Interface (UI) Module gets a query from a user and presents the user the search results from the Ranker. When the UI Module obtains a query from a user, it passes the query to the Web Analyzer and Database. The Web analyzer extracts the web search result from the associated search engine and generates web relevance scores of the returned items. Then, this information is submitted to the

Database. The Database extracts items relevant to the given query and generates their DB relevance scores. It also extract all information of items extracted by Web Analyzer or Database itself. The information contains item contents, global item authorities and DB and Web relevances. Then, this information is submitted to the Ranker, which requests the CF Module expected ratings of items for the given user. Note that CF Module has its own user rating database. Then, items are sorted based on the ranking scheme the user has requested.

7.2 Features of MAD6

MAD6 provides users three information features; Search, Item Presentation, and Personal User role pages. In Search pages, MAD6 presents two search results for a given query: movie search results and people search results. Search ranking can be personalized if a user logs in the system. The user can choose to rank results according to global MADRank, personalized MADRank,Web relevance, DB relevance, or item authorities. Each returned item shows ratings based of four methods (MADRank, Web relevance, DB relevance and item authorities) and matched _elds against the given query. An example search result is shown in Figure 2. There are two types of Item Presentation pages: movies pages and people (actor and director) pages. Each page shows details of the item (title, synopsis, cast, release date, ratings, posters, etc.) along with two lists of relevant items, one showing neighboring items in the collaboration graph of actors and directors, the other based on similarities inferred from user preferences. The Personal User Pro_le page presents the user personal information such as: What queries has the user submitted most frequently? What movies, actors and directors has the user visited most frequently.

7.3 Test procedure

Our online test consists of 44 Yahoo! employees submitting 180 relevance judgments between October 25 2006 and November 7 2006. Each participant is asked to rate at least 10 movies using MAD6 before they participate in the test. When a user comes to our test demo, the user is asked to either submit any free-form query, or to select one of 60 suggested queries provided by our system. The 60 queries are randomly selected from about 5,000 pre-selected queries, including the 500 most popular movie titles, 1,000 actors and 1,000 characters (the top 2 actors/roles from each of the top 500 most popular movies) and 2,400 randomly selected Yahoo! Search queries that resulted in a click on a movie link (300 randomly selected queries from each day in our data set).

After a participant submits a query, the test demo returns ranked results of six systems: IMDB search, Yahoo! Movies current search, and our four algorithms. The demo does not tell users which result is generated by which system, and the location of each system is randomly selected whenever a query is submitted. After reviewing the six different search results, participants are asked to answer following three questions: (1) Which system or systems _nds the movie most relevant to your query? (2) Overall, which system or systems seems to be the most useful for you? And (3) What movie is most relevant to your query? A participant may select multiple systems for the _rst two questions. The _rst question is asked to measure recall of search results and the second question is asked to measure quality of search results. The third question requires a free form text answer.

7.4 Test results

In general, we _nd that Web, GRank and PRank perform better than IMDB, current Yahoo! Movies, and DB, as shown in Table 7. PRank performs best on recall while GRank performs best on quality of search results when all 180 relevance judgments are analyzed. We also classify queries by comparing them with the user's stated target movie (question 3). If a query exactly matches with the title of the target movie, we consider it a navigational query. Otherwise, we consider it an informational query. This classi_cation is manually done by the _rst author. We classify 49 queries as navigational queries. A feature of IMDB search hampers our ability to evaluate IMBD results for navigational queries. For exact title matches, IMDB often (but not always) returns the inferred target movie page directly, rather than listing one or more movies on a search results page. Our wrapper did not properly handle this case

and the online test showed empty results for IMDB when this happened. Thus, we exclude IMDB when results of navigational queries are evaluated. Note that we did make the proper correction for the o_ine test in the previous section. When navigational queries are submitted, PRank performs best while DB performs worst both on recall and quality of search results. It is somewhat surprising that the recall of most systems remains about 50 _ 60% even when the titles of the target movie is submitted as a query. We _nd that many participants often check only one system in the _rst question even though all six systems return the target movie, probably because participants either did not inspect results carefully enough or misinterpreted the intent of question 1. Thus, we want to point out that our recall analysis on the online test may contain some noise. When informational queries are submitted, PRank shows the best recall while GRank performs best on quality.

8. CONCLUSIONS

In this paper, we discuss our new ranking method, which combines recommender systems and search tools for better informational search and browsing. To evaluate our approach, we have built MAD6, a personalized movie search engine with some unique features. In both o_ine and online tests, MAD6 seems to provide users better search recall and quality than IMDB search and Yahoo! Movies current search by combining proximities and authorities of the returned. This paper presents novel collaborative filtering algorithms that incorporate SVD approximation technique into an SVD based EM procedure. In centralized recommendation systems, the standard SVD based EM procedure algorithm takes O(m2n + mn2) time for each SVD computation, while our new algorithm with SVD approximation takes only O(s2n) time. Experiments on existing data sets show that our algorithm is very promising. Its prediction accuracy is almost the same as that of the standard algorithm even if a small approximation ratio is used. We also propose a new framework for collaborative filtering *via* SVD approximation in distributed recommendation systems in which the server periodically calculates an aggregate from online users' rating profiles and makes predictions for all users based on it. Our experiments show that if the number of online users is at least five percent of the total number of users, the prediction accuracy in this distributed scenario is almost the same as what is obtained in the centralized scenario. As companies invest in ever-more sophisticated information technologies that allow consumers to actively and passively discover products that they otherwise would not have considered, and as consumers gain more experience using these IT-enabled tools, our findings suggest that product sales will become less and less concentrated. The balance of power will continue to shift from a few best-selling products to niche products that are previously difficult to be discovered by consumers. This Long Tail phenomenon will have a profound impact on a firm's product development strategy, operations strategy, and marketing strategy. Because the underlying technological drivers that we have studied in this paper are certain to continue to progress in advanced economies, the implications of these technologies for firm strategies and economic welfare are likely to become increasingly important.

9. REFERENCES

[1] C. C. Aggarwal, J. L. Wolf, K.-L. Wu, and P. S. Yu. Horting hatches an egg: a new graph-theoretic approach to collaborative _ltering. In ACM KDD, pages 201{212, 1999.

[2] M. Balabanovic and Y. Shoham. Fab: content-based, collaborative recommendation. Communications of the ACM, 40(3):66{72, 1997.

[3] J. Basilico and T. Hofmann. Unifying collaborative and content-based _ltering. In ICML, 2004.

[4] D. Billsus and M. J. Pazzani. Learning collaborative information _lters. In ICML, pages 46{54, 1998.

[5] J. S. Breese, D. Heckerman, and C. Kadie. Empirical analysis of predictive algorithms for collaborative _ltering. In UAI, pages 43{52, 1998.

[6] M. Claypool, A. Gokhale, T. Miranda, P. Murnikov, D. Netes, and M. Sartin. Combining content-based and collaborative _lters in an online newspaper. In ACM SIGIR Workshop on Recommender Systems, 1999.

[7] D. DeCoste. Collaborative prediction using ensembles of maximum margin matrix f actorization. In ICML, 2006.

[8] M. Deshpande and G. Karypis. Item-based top-n recommendation algorithms. ACM TOIS, 22(1):143{177, Jan 2004.

[9] D. Goldberg, D. Nichols, B. Oki, and D. Terry. Using collaborative _ltering to weave an information tapestry. Communications of the ACM, 35(12):61{70, 1992.

[10] K. Goldberg, T. Roeder, D. Gupta, and C. Perkins. Eigentaste: A constant time collaborative _ltering algorithm. Information Retrieval, 4(2):133{151, 2001.

[11] J. L. Herlocker, J. A. Konstan, A. Borchers, and J. Riedl. An algorithmic framework for performing collaborative filtering. In *Proceedings of the 22nd ACM SIGIR Conference*, 1999.

[12] B. Marlin and R. S. Zemel. The multiple multiplicative factor model for collaborative filtering. In *Proceedings of the 21st International Conference on Machine learning*, 2004.

[13] D. M. Pennock, E. Horvitz, S. Lawrence, and C. L. Giles. Collaborative filtering by personality diagnosis: A hybrid memory and model-based approach. In *Proceedings of the 16th Conference on Uncertainty in Artificial Intelligence*, 2000.

[14] P. Resnick, N. Iacovou, M. Suchak, P. Bergstorm, and J. Riedl. GroupLens: An Open Architecture for Collaborative Filtering of Netnews. In *Proceedings of ACM Conference on Computer Supported Cooperative Work*, 1994.

[15] B. M. Sarwar, G. Karypis, J. A. Konstan, and J. Riedl. Application of dimensionality reduction in recommender systems–a case study. In *ACM WebKDD Web Mining for E-Commerce Workshop*, 2000.

[16] N. Srebro and T. Jaakkola. Weighted low rank approximation. In *Proceedings of the 20th International Conference on Machine Learning*, 2003.

[17] B. Marlin. Collaborative _ltering: A machine learning perspective. Master's thesis, University of Toronto, Computer Science Department, 2004.

[18] P. Melville, R. Mooney, and R. Nagarajan. Content-boosted collaborative _ltering. In AAAI, 2002.

[19] L. Page, S. Brin, R. Motwani, and T. Winograd. The pagerank citation ranking: Bringing order to the web. Technical report, Stanford Digital Library Technologies Project, 1998.

[20] S.-T. Park, D. M. Pennock, and D. DeCoste. Applying collaborative _ltering techniques to movie search for better ranking and browsing. In ITWP, 2006.

[21] S.-T. Park, D. M. Pennock, O. Madani, N. Good, and D. DeCoste. Na__ve _lterbots for robust cold-start recommendations. In KDD, 2006.

[22] D. Pennock, E. Horvitz, S. Lawrence, and C. L. Giles. Collaborative _ltering by personality diagnosis: A hybrid memory- and model-based approach. In UAI, pages 473{480, 2000.

[23] A. Popescul, L. Ungar, D. Pennock, and S. Lawrence. Probabilistic models for uni_ed collaborative and content-based recommendation in sparse-data environments. In UAI, pages 437{444, 2001.

[24] J. Rennie and N. Srebro. Fast maximum margin matrix factorization for collaborative prediction. In ICML, 2005.

[25] P. Resnick, N. Iacovou, M. Suchak, P. Bergstorm, and J. Riedl. GroupLens: An Open Architecture for Collaborative Filtering of Netnews. In ACM CSCW, pages 175{186, 1994.

[26] B. Sarwar, G. Karypis, J. Konstan, and J. Riedl. Application of dimensionality reduction in recommender systems{a case study. In ACM WebKDD Workshop, 2000.

[27] B. M. Sarwar, G. Karypis, J. A. Konstan, and J. Reidl. Item-based collaborative _ltering recommendation algorithms. In WWW, pages 285{295, 2001.

[28] U. Shardanand and P. Maes. Social information _ltering: Algorithms for automating "word of mouth". In CHI, 1995.